The Flower Arranger's Garden

Patricia R. Barrett

The flower arranger is an artist whose materials are those things that grow around him or her. Choosing and growing your own materials can be as creative an experience as making the finished arrangement.

Successful flower arranging and gardening for arranging take practice and experimentation. But once you have tried it you'll be thrilled to have a work of art on display in your home — your own arrangement.

Growing your own plant material for flower arrangements allows you to plan ahead. With some forethought, you can grow certain flowers for a special event such as a wedding or a flower show, have enough foliage for large arrangements, and decorate your home year round with bouquets of homegrown flowers.

A flower arranger's garden does not, however, have to be large. A garden can be created on a small scale that will give you flowers and foliage throughout the year. Trees, shrubs, edging plants, and even herb and vegetable gardens can be planted with a flower arrangement in mind. Chive flowers dry beautifully and work well in small bouquets. A few leaves of a red lettuce can be tucked into a bowl of green Envy zinnias for a striking, and maybe ribbon-winning, arrangement.

Before planting something you should consider not only how it will look in the garden but also how it will do when cut and brought into the house. In addition, there are other questions to consider when choosing a plant:

— Does it flower?
— When will it bloom?
— What is its lasting quality when cut?
— Is it fragrant?
— Is it available during the barren seasons?
— Does it have a good form or color when viewed up close?
— Does it have interesting branches or foliage?
— Can it be dried or preserved for continuous use?
— Will its color work in the home and with the other plants already in the garden?

At first, this thought process seems odd to some gardeners, but once accustomed to considering plants in this manner, the question, "How will it look in an arrangement?" comes naturally. Not all of the plants you grow will be suitable for cutting. Some flowers won't take up water and will quickly wilt when placed in a vase of water. (Sometimes, however, the container you want to use will be the problem. It may have too slim a neck or not enough space for water).

In planning your garden you may first want to consider what already grows around your home. If there are evergreens planted near the house, you may have enough foliage for winter arrangements. Perhaps you have lilacs for May bloom and need color in July and August. Or, you have only yellow flowers in a perennial border and yellow is the one color that does not work in your peach living room. Make a list of the kind of plant material you already have and another list of what you would like to have. Then, think about where you could plant this.

Whether you have room for an entirely new garden or just a few new shrubs, the style of your home will help dictate what to plant. Plants selected for containers on an apartment rooftop might be very different from those suitable for a seaside backyard or a country house surrounded by meadows. A city home may want more formal flowers, a seaside cottage may like roses to mix with shells, and a country house may need only foliage plants in the garden to combine with neighboring wildflowers.

Design principles apply to landscaping projects as well as to flower arrangements. Each composition should have the same characteristics: *balance*, a proper size relationship of all the parts to each other and to the composition as a whole, *contrast*, for the sake of interest, rhythm and harmony, and the proper *scale*, or size and proportion.

When selecting plants for your garden, think of these design principles and of the questions previously listed. If you do, the plants you choose will more than likely work well together when picked and placed in that tall art deco vase your great-aunt Sally gave you. Some plants will work better than others. Don't be afraid to experiment and to change the garden after it's been planted. Some plants, especially in a small garden, will spread too freely and take up space that could be better used by something else.

Trees and Shrubs

Trees and shrubs are the backbone of every garden and can provide excellent foliage for flower arrangements. They are also very useful in the autumn, winter and early spring when there isn't much else in the garden. Since they will probably be the biggest plants in your garden, it is wise to consider them first.

If your garden is small you will have to be careful of the eventual size of the plants you choose. The small yew purchased at the nursery today might take over the garden in five years and have to be pulled out. In addition to size, check the plant's hardiness, freedom from disease and ease of growth. And — something that is often overlooked — what does the plant look like in each season? Is a lack of flowers more than offset by brilliant red foliage in the fall? Does it have berries that last all winter long? Is it deciduous? Is the foliage variegated or plain? Is the bark interesting? Do the branches grow in a curving pattern?

Trees

There are many excellent specimen trees that do well in arrangements. The flowering cherries, crabapples, dogwoods, magnolias, hollies, and birches (with their wonderful bark), are dramatic accents in a garden as well as later in a mixed arrangement. The miniature red-leafed Japanese maple has foliage that is worthwhile, and is small enough so that it can easily be placed into many different garden plots.

Some trees to consider for planting in an arranger's garden are:

MAPLE *(Acer* species). There are many forms of this deciduous tree that do well in most parts of the country. The smaller varieties are good for the arranger, as the leaves in autumn, and in some varieties all year round, can provide excellent color in arrangements. The Japanese maple *(Acer palmatum)* can grow to about 20 feet and is hardy in most areas except the extreme north. All varieties need good soil to grow; some will retain the red or yellow color of the foliage throughout the year. Another popular variety is the threadleaf Japanese maple *(A. palmatum dissectum)*. This has finely cut, blood red leaves and graceful branches. Its leaves, mixed with a few pale pink peonies, are delightful.

DOGWOOD *(Cornus* species) is an excellent choice if the arranger's garden isn't too far north, though some cultivars can withstand cold temperatures and brisk winds. Dogwoods prefer a rich soil in either sun or shade. The variety *C. alba* 'Sibirica' has brilliant red stems which can be used in striking winter flower arrangements. *C. kousa* and the less hardy *C. kousa chinensis* are bushy plants whose flower bracts are pointed at the tip.

CHERRY *(Prunus* species) comes in many different varieties. Those in the *Prunus serrulata* group grow to 25 feet, with single or double, pink or white flowers that bloom early, before the leaves appear. Check for hardiness for your area. *P. yedoensis* grows to about 48 feet and is a very attractive tree with graceful branches and slightly fragrant white to pink flowers. This is the tree planted in the greatest numbers around the Washington D.C. tidal basin.

Shrubs

Shrubs are good choices since they can be used as the framework of many floral arrangements. In the fall or winter, a few branches of a dark green yew or a lighter juniper in a vase with one or two purchased flowers will easily lift your spirits, and won't be too hard on your budget since the basis of the arrangement is already in the garden.

There is a wide selection of shrubs for a mixed garden border. Some can go almost unnoticed in a garden but are handsome additions to a flower arrangement. These include cotoneaster, spirea, potentilla and the dwarf hollies. Other shrubs are more dramatic and won't recede into the background. These include many of the azaleas, the viburnums, *Enkianthus campanulatus* (with its autumn foliage), the many forms of euonymus, pyracantha (with its orange-red berries) and many of the dark green yews and silver-gray junipers. Underneath shrubs is a good location for groundcovers such as pachysandra, vinca and ivy, which are essential. A bowl filled with pachysandra can be a long-lasting base for many future flower arrangements.

Hedges are something else to think about. You can grow such delights as forsythia, bush honeysuckle *(Lonicera* species), the old-fashioned mock orange, the *rugosa* roses (which have large hips in the late summer and fall), and many of the *Syringa* species, including the common lilac.

There are numerous shrubs that work well in a garden and are excellent for the flower arrangement. The choice depends on the arranger's needs which may be foliage, early spring bloom, winter berries, or perhaps all of these.

Shrub varieties to consider:

BARBERRY *(Berberis* species) would not be considered by some arrangers to be a good garden choice but some of the varieties, with their purplish leaves and rapid growth, make a fine addition to the garden if you have the space. The Japanese barberry *(B. thunbergii)* is very easy to grow and keeps its red berries all winter long, which is a plus for the arranger.

BUTTERFLY BUSH *(Buddleia* species) has very fragrant blossoms and naturally curving stems which provide needed line in flower arrangements. *B. alternifolia* is a hardy variety with small, lavender flowers. *B davidii magnifica,* the oxeye butterfly bush, is commonly grown in the United States. Its flowers are dark blue with orange eyes.

BOX or boxwood *(Buxus* species) is a wonderful shrub for both the garden and the arrangement, provided it will grow in your area. The English box *(B. sempervirens)* and its many varieties are not considered hardy north of Zone 6. There are miscellaneous seedlings of some boxes that are considered hardy. Look for locally grown plants that will be hardy in the area where you live. Perhaps you'll stumble on a yet-unnamed variety which will work. Box foliage is extremely long-lasting in a flower arrangement and attractive for background filler.

CYPRESS *(Chamaecyparis* species) is an evergreen with flat branches and small cones. Many of the cultivars have excellent spraylike foliage that can be used all year long for background and to hide mechanics in a flower arrangement. It grows well in rich, moist soils and does not like dry or windy areas of the garden. It may not be hardy in some northern areas. Cultivars of *C. lawsoniana* (hardy to Zone 5) are good to look for.

BROOM *(Cytisus* species) is almost a must in the flower arranger's garden, not only for its myriad blossoms in different colors, but for its stems, which can be curved and dried into pleasing shapes for arrangements. The only problem with broom is that it is rarely hardy north of Boston. Some varieties will survive in the north with protection or in locations near the coast. The branches may be picked in the winter and look lovely alone as well as mixed with other flowers for an elegant line arrangement. *C. scoparius* (Scotch broom) is a native to Great Britain and has become naturalized in many parts of this country. It has masses of yellow flowers in the early summer and its many hybrids have flowers in different colors. *C. praecox* (Warminster broom) is a bit hardier than *C. scoparius,* and has yellow flowers and evergreen branches.

EUCALYPTUS *(Eucalyptus* species) provides gray foliage to those lucky enough to be in the warm climates where it grows. Its leaves absorb glycerine easily, keep their color well, and even when dried look fine with fresh flowers.

EUONYMUS *(Euonymus* species) is the one plant that could be considered a must for the arranger's garden. It comes in many varieties and can be grown as a shrub, tree, or rapidly growing groundcover or vine. Its foliage is long lasting when cut and is great filler or base material for many arrangements. It comes in all-green or variegated forms. *E. fortunei* is very hardy with leathery, glossy green leaves. It has many cultivars with different colored leaves and growth habits. *E. japonica* is not as hardy but has many popular variegated varieties, such as *E. japonica albomarginata,* whose leaves have a thin rim of white around the edge.

FORSYTHIA *(Forsythia* species) can grow to absurd heights of over 12 feet and can get just as wide, but its early yellow blossoms are easy to force indoors and are such a welcome sign of spring that most gardeners find a spot for it. Forsythias do well in most any soil but they do prefer the sun for early flowering. 'Lynwood Gold' and 'Beatrix Farrand' are classic cultivars, with the latter getting somewhat taller. Both have lots of large, bright yellow flowers.

WITCH HAZEL *(Hamamelis* species) has feathery flowers on its stems and makes a simple arrangement with little else added. *H. virginiana* blooms late in the fall, which is a plus. Others bloom very early in the year, sometimes in February or March, before the leaves appear. For this reason alone, it is a useful plant. *H. mollis* is a popular witch hazel with yellow flowers from winter to spring and yellow leaves in the fall.

HOLLY *(Ilex* species), where it is hardy, is an excellent choice for the arranger's border. It is traditional for winter arrangements. It is very long lasting once picked and placed in water and looks well with most flowers. *Ilex aquifolium* is the common holly and the parent of many useful cultivars.

MOCK ORANGE *(Philadelphus* species) has many uses in the garden, is very hardy and has fragrant blooms in midsummer. There are many varieties of *Philadelphus* that work well in a garden and in an arrangement.

RHODODENDRONS and AZALEAS *(Rhododendron* species) come in many varieties perfect for an arranger's garden. One has only to think of a color and then select the perfect shade. Some azaleas will not be hardy in the north, and they like lime-free soils. If you can grow them you will be rewarded with fine materials for flower arranging.

LILAC *(Syringa* species) comes in many varieties in addition to the common lilac, *Syringa vulgaris*. There is a wide range of colors available, from deep purple to pale pink and clear white. Choose a plant that will go with your color scheme and will work with the rest of the plants in the garden. Perhaps you would prefer a pink lilac to the more usual lavender, or one of the later-blooming Korean lilacs, with more delicate blossoms and a lovely scent. A few lilac blooms mixed with their own dark green leaves and set in a white or covered pitcher always looks good almost anywhere in the house.

VIBURNUM *(Viburnum* species) is one of the best shrubs for a flower arranger because it has flowers, winter berries and distinctive foliage. Among the many varieties to choose from are *V. plicatum* (Japanese snowball), *V. prunifolium,* with flat clusters of white flowers and black fruits, and *V. carlessii* (fragrant viburnum), with a delightful scent.

Flowers

No matter how many arrangements you put together over the years, you never tire of flowers. Their endless forms, textures, colors and scents are what first inspire you to cut them and bring them inside so you can enjoy their loveliness all over again. So once trees and shrubs are selected for your yard, you will want to add the annuals, perennials and bulbs for the variety that only flowers can give. One of the most important parts of your plan is to ensure continuous bloom throughout the season, beginning as early as you can, with spring tulips and daffodils, and continuing through the fall, with chrysanthemums and late bloomers such as *Helenium.*

Seed catalogs are a good place to start when planning a cutting garden. Look for plants that are labeled "good for cutting." This usually means that the flower will hold up well after it has been cut. Flowers with long, firm stems are good, though weaker stems can be strengthened later by the addition of a thin florist's wire. Avoid flowers that fade quickly or fall apart soon after cutting. Sometimes you won't know this until you've tried them out one year.

A garden doesn't have to be big to provide lots of bloom. For small yards, one single, wide, interrelated plan can be effective. A border 5 feet wide and 10 feet long can work just fine for starters.

A common gardening mistake is to plant just one of a variety and then wonder what happened to it when it seems to disappear in a surrounding sea of green. Plant at least 3 plants of the same variety in a group to make a distinctive showing of color and to give you enough to cut. If you have enough space, plant a sweep of 5-7 plants. Repeat the mass of color at intervals the whole length of the border. In between these masses, use complementary colors or, if you want just pink (or any other color) flowers, use darker and lighter shades of that color in the garden.

Next, think of the form of the flower. You don't want only round, daisylike forms, but rather a mix of textures and shapes to provide interest in the garden and later in flower arrangements.

When you go a step beyond merely picking flowers for home arrangements and begin to think about entering flower shows, your planning takes on new importance. Now you think about what kind of arrangement you may be doing for a show and plant accordingly. If you are lucky enough to have the show schedule (which describes the different classes in the show) before planting time, all the better. Then you'll know ahead of time what to grow. For example, a show may have a class in it called "winter whites," which calls for a monochromatic arrangement depicting the cold season we are all too familiar with. So, you might look through the seed catalog and choose an exotic white flower, maybe a white lily. Or, if it is too late to start your own plants, you'll be able to go to the garden shop and pick out white annuals that would do well.

Annuals

An annual plant is one which develops from seed, flowers, and produces more seeds before dying, all in the period of one year. They have a long period of bloom and bloom more abundantly the more they are cut, features which make them the mainstay of a good cutting garden. They are also easy to grow, fairly free of disease, and come in a wide variety of shapes and colors. Annuals can be tucked in between perennials, shrubs, or even vegetables. Or, they can have their own space, a bed apart from the rest. They're most adaptable.

Since annuals are in the garden for a short period of time, you do not have to prepare the soil too deeply. Any well-drained soil will do. Some seedlings can be started directly in the garden. Others have to be started indoors and then moved to the garden after danger of frost has passed. Proper spacing (depending on the size of the grown plant) is required, and weeding is necessary as the plant grows. Cut off any spent blooms to encourage further flowering. Annuals may need some liquid fertilizer during the growing season but most don't need to be fed frequently.

The list of annuals is long. Try anything that appeals to you. One to start from seed is salpiglossis or velvet flower. Its trumpet-shaped blossoms give a certain elegant touch to an otherwise simple arrangement. Others are asters, nasturtiums (with sunny leaves and bright blooms), petunias, cleome, and the daisy-type flowers, such as *Helianthus*. Others, not quite annuals, but grown as such, include the gladioli, in unusual colors, and the dahlias. Other annuals to try in your arranging garden include:

SNAPDRAGON *(Antirrhinum* species). These tall, pointed flower stalks are excellent in flower arrangements, giving good form and line to many styles. They come in a wide variety of colors and are easily grown in light, rather rich soils in full sun. Start these seeds indoors, and place the plants in the garden at least 15 inches apart. They will flower all season.

CALENDULA *(Calendula officinalis)*. This hardy annual is easy to grow. It comes in shades of orange, yellow and cream, and holds up well in flower arrangements. Its rough texture makes it ideal for casual arrangements such as might be made in baskets or pottery bowls.

CALLIOPSIS, or annual coreopsis *(Coreopsis* species). These small, long-lasting flowers come in shades of yellow, orange, deep mahogany and crimson. They look good even after all the petals have fallen off! Their brown stigmas and feathery foliage are delightful. They are easy to grow from seed.

COSMOS *(Cosmos* species). The different forms of cosmos are attractive and long lasting when cut. Some of the tall-growing varieties need plenty of room to grow but the smaller ones can fit in most anywhere. If kept cut, they will bloom all summer long. Good single color varieties include the clear white 'Sensation' cosmos or the brilliant red *C. sulphureus* 'Diablo.' A dainty newer variety is *C. bipinnatus* 'Candy Stripe,' with white flowers edged in crimson. Cosmos starts easily from seed and likes a poor soil. If the soil is too rich you are likely to get lush foliage and small flowers. Sow seed indoors in the spring or directly in the garden.

FLOWERING TOBACCO *(Nicotiana* species). These tube-shaped, starlike flowers come in a number of colors, including a lime green that is effective in flower arrangements. Nicotiana can be used in both formal and informal flower arrangements. Seeds should be started indoors and plants may be grown in full sun or part shade, spaced about 12 inches apart.

MARIGOLD *(Tagetes* species). Some people don't grow marigolds for arrangements, saying they are too common and don't add anything to a floral display. But marigolds, if chosen for color and style, can add long-lasting, colorful blooms to many casual bouquets. Some forms are large chrysanthemum types, while others are small and airier. They are all easy to grow and are best started indoors and moved to the garden. When cut, they need a lot of water.

ZINNIA *(Zinnia* species). These in all their varieties are fundamental for an arranger's garden. The single-color varieties rather than the mixed will enable you to grow the specific colors you want. The distinctive apple green color of the Envy zinnia always looks good when picked and added to a bouquet. Cut-and-come-again zinnias are good because they do just as their name indicates. Zinnias like full sun and rich soil to which compost or manure has been added. They start easily from seed sown directly in the garden or earlier indoors.

Perennials

There are so many perennials, it's difficult to begin. But how can you resist? If you had to choose you might include yarrow, astilbe and heliopsis for their constant bloom. Other musts include irises, delphiniums for their grandeur, and all the veronicas and salvias. Extras would be the perennial asters, *Helenium* for the early fall, feverfew, the alliums, monkshood, baby's breath and all the lilies. Biennials to include would be foxglove and Sweet William. Lavender makes a good edging plant and its silvery leaves and purple, spiked flowers are excellent in a small arrangement. All the silvery artemisias are good additions. Their foliage holds up well and mixes nicely with many flowers. Hosta is a good choice for a shady spot. Although it is difficult to choose from the many varieties that are excellent for arrangements, here are a few to get started with:

YARROW *(Achillea* species). Yarrow is easy to grow and prefers a sunny spot in the garden. Its feathery foliage has a pungent odor and the plants flower throughout the summer and into the fall. Yarrow is available with yellow, white and red flowers. All dry well and may be used in dried as well as fresh arrangements. Some varieties to grow include *A. filipendulina* 'Coronation Gold,' with lemon yellow flowers, and *A. millefolium* 'Red Beauty,' whose rosy flowers fade to pink and white as they grow.

MONKSHOOD *(Aconitum* species) is a beautiful flower for arrangements where blue is needed. Monkshood is a poisonous plant, however, so wash your hands after handling it. *A. napellus* 'Bressingham Spire' has violet-blue flowers on 3-foot spikes. *A. napellus* 'Album' has white flowers. They grow best in damp shade, but will grow in sun if kept moist.

LADY'S MANTLE *(Alchemilla* species) has clusters of unusual greenish or yellowish flowers that stand above the leaves and last a long time in water. The leaves also work well in arrangements. A good variety is *A. vulgaris,* with large, roundish leaves. It does well in sun or partial shade and ordinary garden soil.

COLUMBINE *(Aquilegia* species) makes excellent cut flowers and lovely border plants, blooming for 4-6 weeks beginning in early June. The color range of the flowers covers pink, blue, yellow, red and white. The hybrids to try include *A.* 'Langdon's Rainbow Hybrids,' *A. chrysantha* 'Crimson Star' (with long crimson spurs) and *A. chrysantha* 'Silver Queen' (pure white). Columbines are easy to grow from seed and prefer a cool, well-drained spot in partial shade or sun.

ARTEMISIA *(Artemisia* species) may be grown for its silver-gray foliage which looks pretty arranged with pink or blue flowers. *A. ludoviciana* 'Silver Queen' is good for the border and easy to grow in well-drained soil, in full sun or partial shade.

ASTILBE *(Astilbe* species) has feathery, plumed spikes that grow above its ferny foliage. It likes fertile, moist soil with quite a bit of organic matter in it. Both flowers and leaves are excellent in arrangements, and very long lasting. The flowers also air dry well. Varieties to try include *A.* x *arendsii* 'Avalanche' (white flowers), *A.* x *arendsii 'Ostrich Plume'* *(salmon-pink flowers),* and *A. taquetii* 'Superba' (good-sized, bright pink plumes).

BELLFLOWER *(Campanula* species) blends well with other

garden flowers in mass arrangements. Choose varieties with long stems, such as *C. persicifolia* 'Grandiflora Alba' with white flowers on 2-foot stalks, and *C. persicifolia* 'Telham Beauty,' with blue flowers. They do well in sun, in a fertile soil with a dressing of lime, if needed.

CHRYSANTHEMUMS *(Chrysanthemum* species) make excellent cut flowers and are invaluable for autumn arrangements. There are numerous varieties to choose from. Look for those in colors that will work well in your home. *C. maximum* is the favorite Shasta daisy which works well in so many arrangements and looks lovely in a garden border.

PYRETHRUM *(Chrysanthemum coccineum)* has daisylike flowers of bright pink or red. The flowers are very useful and work well in informal arrangements or used as a filler. They are easy to grow in sandy or loamy soil and like full sun. Try 'Robinson's Rose' for pink-rose flowers.

COREOPSIS *(Coreopsis* species). The lovely daisylike yellow of flowers of *C. grandiflora* have long, sturdy stems and make excellent, long-lasting cut flowers. Coreopsis likes a sunny location and will do well in any well-drained soil. *C. verticillata* 'Grandiflora' has finely cut leaves and yellow flowers on 2-foot stems. *C. lanceolata* 'Brown Eyes' or the double 'New Gold' has yellow flowers that are excellent in mixed casual arrangements.

DELPHINIUM *(Delphinium* species) is an ideal outline material for very large arrangements. If your garden has the space, try a few of these tall-growing perennials. They are somewhat difficult to grow and require fertile soil, winter protection, and staking. There are many varieties; among the best is the Blackmore and Langdon strain, with large flowers and strong spikes. Though delphiniums are known best for their blue and purple shades, there are lovely pinks and whites to choose from as well.

DORONICUM *(Doronicum cordatum)* is an early-spring-flowering plant with yellow dailylike flowers. It is worth including in the garden for it looks lovely in a bouquet with red tulips and yellow narcissus. It goes dormant in the summer but is easy to grow in moist soil in either full or partial sun.

GAILLARDIA *(Gaillardia* species) is a useful cutting flower, with bright blooms on sturdy stems. The daisylike flowers like a rich soil in full sun and will bloom all summer long if kept cut. Varieties to try include *G.* x *grandiflora* 'Burgundy' and 'Monarch Strain.'

BABY'S BREATH *(Gypsophila paniculata)* is used a great deal, both fresh and dried, in arrangements. Its starlike, small flowers add a light, airy touch to many arrangements and are good filler for those holes in masses of flowers. White is the usual color, though a pale pink is also useful. It prefers a well-drained, rich soil and does not like to be moved once established. It needs to be staked to keep it from sprawling in the garden. 'Bristol Fairy' and 'Perfecta' are good white versions of this perennial; 'Pink Fairy' is a pink.

CORAL BELLS *(Heuchera sanguinea)* are lovely, long-lasting cut flowers and can be used to establish height in arrangements. The stems are slender but strong, and can be gently curved. The foliage is also useful in small arrangements. Coral bells is low growing and works well as an edging plant. It is easy to grow and will do well in sun or partial shade. *H. sanguinea* has crimson-red flowers that bloom from June to September. *H. sanguinea* 'White Cloud' is the white form.

HOSTA *(Hosta* species) is grown for both its leaves and flowers. The flowers are long lasting and work well in masses of pastels, and the leaves can be used all summer long in all types of arrangements. There are many forms and sizes of hostas, some with pale green solid-color leaves, others with variegated leaves. Use 1 or 2 leaves in the early spring with a few flowers and you can easily have an effective arrangement. Hosta is easy to grow in ordinary soil but it prefers shady sites.

IRIS *(Iris* species) is an excellent flower for early spring arrangements. Three irises with their foliage can make a simple yet elegant picture. There are many types of iris, from the large bearded varieties to the simple Siberian and Japanese irises. If you have the space you may want to plant many different kinds. If your garden is small, consider at least one variety for spring flowers. Choose a color you like, perhaps a pale blue, a deep purple or a pure white.

LILIES *(Lilium* species) are all lovely and make wonderful focal points for any flower arrangement. They can be elegant or simple, depending on which flowers are combined with them. One beautiful lily used by itself with a stalk of broom can be enough for an arrangement. Look for long-stemmed lilies in colors that go with the rest of your color scheme. They prefer filtered light and good air circulation, and can be planted in the fall or early spring. When you cut them, remove the stamens to prevent the inner surface of the flower from being marked by pollen.

BEE BALM *(Monarda didyma)* has a showy flower that looks best in informal arrangements. 'Cambridge Scarlet' has brilliant red blooms and 'Croftway Pink' has light salmon-pink flowers. They are easy to grow but are invasive; if you have the space they are worth the room.

PEONY *(Paeonia* species). If you have room for just one peony be sure to plant it, for the foliage is long lasting and can be used as a base for arrangements all summer long. The back of a peony leaf, with its silver-gray cast, can be used as often as the darker green side. The flowers are elegant and rich looking, and the effect of a few massed in a bowl or just one floating in a dish of water are reason enough for this long-living plant. You may choose the double-flowered peonies or the single, more elegant, and Oriental-looking types. They like rich soil in full sun and a lot of space, as they become quite bushy when fully grown.

PHLOX *(Phlox* species) are old-fashioned flowers that look best in mixed summer bouquets. They like rich soil, and planting a few different varieties will help ensure blooms all summer long. Choose colors you like in the light pink or white range. Don't let them go to seed in the garden, as their seedlings tend to be a magenta color of little use.

SALVIA *(Salvia* species) comes in many forms and its chief value is the long life of the cut flowers. The taller varieties provide an arrangement with excellent outline. *S. haematodes* is a tall plant with lavender-blue flowers, and *S.* x *superba* has branching spikes of violet-blue flowers, and tends to be shorter.

PINCUSHION FLOWER *(Scabiosa* species) comes in shades of blue that are most useful to a flower arranger. The long stems make them good choices and they look good growing in the garden. They prefer a well-drained, light soil in full sun. *S. caucasica* grows to about 24 inches and blooms all summer.

VERONICA *(Veronica* species) is valuable to the arranger for its many spiked flowers which last all summer and dry well. Some of the deepest blues come in this flower, and other colors range from white to pinks and purples. *V. latifolia* 'Crater Lake Blue' is 12–18 inches tall with true blue flowers. *V. spicata* has many cultivars worthy of cutting, including 'Red Fox,' with rosy flowers, and 'Blue Peter,' with deep blue blooms. Veronica is easy to grow in any well-drained soil, in either sun or partial shade.

Drying and Preserving Flowers

In addition to the flowers that can be picked and used right away in delightful arrangements, there are many flowers that are better for arranging when dried or preserved. Many garden flowers and wildflowers may be dried by using a dessicant or by hanging them upside down to air dry, but some flowers tolerate it better than others.

Drying Agents

Dessicant comes in 3 forms: borax, sand or a silica gel, all of which absorb moisture from the flower. Different mixtures to try are: borax; half borax and half corn meal; half borax and half white silica builder's sand; fine white builder's sand; and "Flower Dri" and similar products. Many different flowers may be dried using this method. Its benefit is that the flower's color is preserved well. Its disadvantage is that it is rather time consuming, and the boxes filled with the drying agent can take up quite a bit of room. Dessicants are probably the best way to preserve those special blooms of roses, daffodils and zinnias. Any garden flower may be tried.

SOME WILDFLOWERS THAT DRY WELL WITHOUT USING A DESSICANT

Bergamot	Milkweed
Black-eyed Susan	Mullein
Butterfly weed	Pearly everlasting
Cattail	Pussy willow
Dock	Tansy
Goldenrod	Teasel
Joe-Pye weed	

Plants with attractive seed pods for dried arrangements:

Bittersweet	Honesty
Chinese lantern	Iris
Columbine	Lily
Delphinium	Poppy
Globe thistle	Conifers

The process is simple enough. Cut the flowers on a sunny day before they have reached full maturity and when the colors are clear and true. Strip the leaves from the stalks and place the stalks lengthwise in a box of the dessicant. Round flowers such as zinnias, chrysanthemums, marigolds and anemones should be placed face down. Cover the flowers gently with more of the mixture.

PLANTS AND FLOWERS FOR HANGING

Achillea — These flowers will dry on the plant, but may be hung to dry.
Artemisia
Globe amaranth
Baby's breath
Bells of Ireland
Delphinium
Fern fronds
Globe thistle (*Echinops* species) — The mature flowers dry well when hung or placed in a glycerine solution.
Lavender
Sage
Sea lavender (*Limonium* species) — Cut the stems when the flowers are mature and hang in a warm room for 2-4 weeks. Its colors preserve well.
Strawflower (*Helichrysum* species) is excellent when dried for winter. The flowers will dry naturally on the plant but you may want to pick them before they fully mature. Pick the flower heads and immediately mount them on florist's wire. Insert the wire in the top of the flower and hook it behind the petals. Then either hang them upside down or push them into a block of Oasis to dry, which usually takes 3-4 weeks.
Xeranthemum dries very well. The small flowers come in light pink shades. Dry them away from bright light to keep their color.

Glycerine

Glycerine is an excellent material used to preserve foliage for arranging. In this simple process the stems are placed in a glass jar to a depth of 3 inches in a solution of glycerine ($1/3$ glycerine to $2/3$ water). Keep the jar in a cool room and check the foliage every day. When it is pliable, remove the stems and lay them in a box to dry. To store the dried branches you can place them in a box lined with newspaper or keep them upright in a container. Beech leaves, Elaeagnus, holly, magnolia and oak preserve well in glycerine.

Everlastings

The avid arranger, in an effort to have blooms to use throughout the year, will try to dry everything in the garden, with different degrees of success. With some forethought a garden may have some space devoted to plants called everlastings, so-named for their best quality. Dried arrangements are lovely throughout the year and are easy to do, but they usually need twice the amount of material that a fresh arrangement requires. Also, to avoid all-brown dried arrangements, some thought must be given to providing colorful blooms that dry well.

The traditional way to dry flowers is to cut them on a dry, sunny day, strip the foliage from the stems, group the stems in small bunches and tie together with a rubber band, and hang them upside down. Choose a spot for drying which is warm, dry and has good air circulation. Hang large or thick stems, such as those of delphinium, separately. The length of drying time depends on the structure of the plant. Plants with thin stems and a thin, papery texture will dry faster than those with thick stems and dense texture. Check the plants often as they dry. Sometimes they look so good hanging together, you can simply move the bunch to your kitchen ceiling and call that an arrangement.

Grasses

Arranging with dried materials doesn't have to be limited to flowers. There are many grasses that not only add a distinctive touch to an arrangement but also look graceful in the garden. Some to include are zebra grass and maiden grass (*Miscanthus* species), purple moor grass (*Molinia caerulea*), and *Pennisetum* species. Look for them in seed catalogs or garden centers. They will do well in any ordinary soil. Many wild grasses can be transplanted into the garden or simply cut for use in arrangements.

The tall heads of grass seed blend well with preserved material. Grasses need almost no conditioning when used fresh. To use them dry, it is sometimes best to leave them in the garden until they have dried naturally before cutting. Or, before fully mature they may be cut (with long stems) and hung to dry in a cool, dark place.

Planning the Garden

An arranging garden does not have to include all of the plants already mentioned. It could have a few of each variety, selected on the basis of their time of bloom, color, foliage and the style of flowers you like best.

A small garden for a flower arranger might include a euonymus (either variegated or plain-leafed), a small juniper, a peony, 3 yarrows, 3 astilbes, 2 coral bells, 3 *Heliopsis*, 3 veronicas, a dozen daffodils, and as many zinnias and cosmos as could be squeezed in between the plants. This would, with the help of things gathered from nearby fields and lots, give the arranger many delightful bouquets throughout the year.

But, if you are blessed with space, your problem may not be deciding what to plant, but rather, knowing when to stop planting. It's difficult, especially when there's a flower show on the calendar. There's always something new to try — a new lily, a bi-color cosmos. And, if you do have the room and the strength to keep creating new flower beds, gardening with arrangements in mind can be a never-ending pursuit.

Garden soil needs to be well prepared. The shrubs and perennials will stay in the garden for a long time and the soil needs deep cultivation to accommodate the root growth of these plants. If the garden is to be planted in new soil, first pick the spot, and sketch the area to scale on graph paper.

In the early spring, or in the fall, outline the garden on the sod. You may outline the bed by using stakes and string, a long garden hose curved to show where you want the garden to be, or by "painting" the intended borders with lime.

Digging the sod is the next step. If you start early — the previous fall, for instance — you can dig the sod, turn it over, and layer various organic materials on top of the overturned sod, creating a mini compost pile.

An alternate method is to remove the sod and then replace the soil with peat moss, lime (if needed), rock phosphate, rotted manure, and compost. The organic matter helps improve soil texture and moisture retention.

Planting

Plant annuals after danger of frost is past. Some annuals may be started directly in the garden, but most are started indoors and planted after a short period of hardening off. Annuals may be placed wherever there is a hole in the planting.

Bare-footed shrubs and trees and perennials should be planted in the dormant season, from late fall until spring. Container-grown plants, which include many of the shrubs and some perennials, may be planted at almost any time of the year, but be sure to keep them well watered during the hot summer. If plants arrive by mail while the ground is too hard or too wet for planting, keep their roots covered with straw or a sheet of plastic to retain moisture. To keep them for a longer time, "heel the plants in" by setting them in a shallow trench, covering the roots with soil, and watering thoroughly. If you want to heel them in for the winter, cover the trunks and lower branches with earth, too.

Few shrubs or trees can stand being waterlogged, nor can they tolerate dry conditions. It is a good idea to add organic matter to the hole before planting. Dig a large enough hole so the plant will fit without any trouble. If stakes are needed, set them in place before planting to avoid damaging the roots. After placing the plant in position, shake it gently back and forth to work the soil down into the roots. Add more soil mixed with compost or rotted manure, and tread on it as you go. Water the plant well. Once planted, add mulch to help retain moisture.

Most perennials need to be cut down in the fall, after the frosts have blackened them, to deter pests. This cleanup process, along with the removal of annuals from the garden and the protection of shrubs from winter damage, is all that is usually needed to "put the garden to bed" for the winter. After a hard frost, when the ground is frozen, a layer of pine or spruce boughs may go over the plants to protect them from alternately freezing and thawing throughout the winter.

In the spring remove the boughs and carefully rake the garden. Then feed either with fertilizer or with your own rich compost. It is also time to replant or rethink the garden and to begin to use it for its original purpose — to fill the house with flower arrangements.

Cutting and Conditioning

Success in flower arranging depends on knowing the best ways to condition and maintain plant materials to keep them looking fresh.

Conditioning is the plant's process of taking on more water than it gives off, so as to put it into a prime state of freshness. It is all-important for creating flower arrangements that will last for more than a day. It is silly to spend all the time it takes to make a lovely arrangement only to have it begin wilting after a few hours because the material wasn't properly conditioned.

The general rules for conditioning most flowers are the same but there are specific things to do for various blooms. One rule is certain, however: it is best to cut plant material in the evening, because sugar has been stored in the plant tissue all day. The next best time to cut is early morning, and the poorest time is in the middle of the day. This means you have to plan ahead.

Flowers should be cut with a sharp knife or a good pair of garden clippers. Cut the stem on a slant and remove all unncessary foliage. As soon as the flower is cut, place the stem up to its neck in a bucket of warm water and place the flowers in a cool room for at least 6 hours or overnight. A darkened room will slow the development of the blooms. Any that you want to open should be placed close to an indirect light source.

Some stems need special treatment. Brittle stems (such as on chrysanthemums) should be broken to expose a greater surface for water intake. Woody stems (such as lilac) should be peeled back and split an inch or so. Milky stems (such as poppies) must be sealed with a match or other flame, or by dipping the end momentarily into boiling water. Milky stems need to be resealed each time they are cut, so they are not suitable for needlepoint holders, which pierce the stem.

Foliage plants should be cut when they are mature. Tender new growth should usually be removed. Most foliage can be

CONDITIONING FLOWERS

Flower	When to Cut	Treatment for Conditioning
Anemone	½ to fully open	Scrape stems
Aster	¾ to fully open	Scrape stems
Azalea	Bud to fully open	Scrape and crush stems
Bachelor's button	½ to fully open	Scrape stems
Bleeding heart	4 or 5 florets open	Scrape stems
Calendula	Fully open	Scrape stems
Carnation	Fully open; snap or break from plant	Scrape stems
Chrysanthemum	Fully open; break off	Scrape or crush stems
Daffodil	As color shows in bud	Cut foliage sparingly and scrape stems
Dahlia	Fully open	Sear stems in flame
Daisy	½ to fully open	Scrape stems or sear in flame
Delphinium	¾ to fully open	Scrape stems, break off top buds
Gladiolus	As second floret opens	Scrape stems
Iris	As first bud opens	Leave foliage, scrape stems
Lilac	½ to fully open	Scrape and crush stems; put wilted branches in very hot water for 1 hour
Lily	As first bud opens	Cut no more than $1/3$ of stem
Marigold	Fully open	Scrape stems
Peony	Bud in color or fully open	Scrape or split stems
Poppy	Night before opening	Sear stems; a drop of wax in heart of flower keeps it open
Rose	As second petal unfurls; cut stem just above a 5-petal leaf	Scrape stems; cut stems again while holding under water
Tulip	Bud to ½ open	Cut foliage sparingly, scrape stems, stand in deep water overnight
Zinnia	Fully open	Sear stems in flame

immersed completely and some must be. Wilted plant material is not necessarily dead; it may be just thirsty. Recut the stems and place in hot water and most will revive. After conditioning, place the plant material in cool water in a cool room.

Some commercial chemical preparations added to the water in which plants are conditioned have value in that they check maturing, nourish plants, sweeten the water and help slow decay. Other tips to keep in mind are: remove the pollen from self-pollinating flowers; cut the stems under water to keep air bubbles from entering (important with roses); put water in the container before you start the arrangement; and cut the stems straight across for needlepoint holders, and on an angle for deep vases.

Many books have detailed lists of different plant materials and how best to condition them for arranging. The following chart will get you started.

Arranging

Flower arrangers, like any artist, can get carried away with their craft. They scour secondhand shops for vases, tubs, jars, pitchers — anything that will hold a bouquet of fresh-picked flowers. But arrangers need more than a vase. There are many devices that make the task of holding flowers where you want them a whole lot easier.

Some items are essential to the art of arranging; others are just handy. All you really need to get started are three or four containers in the basic shapes, an assortment of needlepoint holders (also called pin holders) and other stem-securing equipment, a sharp knife or flower shears, and florist's tape or clay. The following list gives you an idea of what you may like to have. Items preceded by an asterisk are essential.

**Pin holders* come in a variety of sizes and shapes and will last forever.

**Oasis* is used with or without a pin holder to hold the material in an arrangement in place. It can be purchased at your local florist or garden center, comes in block form and may be cut to size with a sharp knife.

Florist's clay is used to secure the holder to the container.
Styrofoam is used for arranging dried material.
Clippers and a *sharp knife* are essential.
Florist's wire is used to wire stems so they will bend.
Florist's tape is used to cover the wire.
Bleach, 1 teaspoon to a quart of water, will keep the water clean and lengthen the life of the arrangement.
Pebbles in different colors and sizes can be used to cover holders.
A *Lazy Susan* is handy to have for turning the arrangement while you work on it.
Stands and *bases* can be used with the container to improve the design.

The Flower Arrangement

There are many types of flower arrangement, ranging from formal styles with strict rules of form and design, to the casual mix of flowers in a basket. The style of an arrangement will more often than not be dictated by the style of one's home. An abstract arrangement might not work well in a home filled with 18th-century English antiques. And a mixed bouquet of zinnias and daisies might not look quite right in a stark white living room.

There are many books on how to arrange flowers so we'll just go over the basics here and let the gardener/arranger go by feel for the rest. If you can trust yourself and what you like, then the arrangement will reflect that. Add to your personal tastes a few of the arranging "basics" and you'll soon feel that you know what you are doing. There are almost no rules that have to be observed, but if you understand some principles of good design it will help provide you with a sense of confidence in what you are doing.

Principles of Design

Proportion. Your flower arrangement is in good proportion when it appears to be the right size for its container. In a tall vase, a general rule of thumb is to have the height of the arrangement equal to 1½–2 times the height of the vase. This rule also holds for wide, horizontal containers, in which the tallest stem should be 1½–2 times the width or diameter of the bowl. This rule, of course, may be broken, but following it when beginning to make flower arrangements can simplify the task.

Balance. Arrangements are said to be balanced when they give a sense of stability, and do not look as if they will tip over, or appear to be lopsided. Symmetrical balance is when both halves of the arrangement are identical or nearly identical. Asymmetrical is when the two halves are not the same, yet they appear to be balanced, or to have equal importance.

Texture. It is a good idea to include contrasting textures in an arrangement. This is not difficult to do. Use glossy foliage with soft flowers, or sleek leaves with rough, ruffled blossoms. Nature has already given us many choices here.

Color. So much can be said about color. Study the color wheel and see how colors work together. Sometimes a flower arrangement can be enhanced by using hues of greater and lesser value in the same color family. Dark colors are usually used well in the base of an arrangement, as they look heavier. Colors are usually related to what's in a room — contrasting or blending in with — and white can work in just about any room.

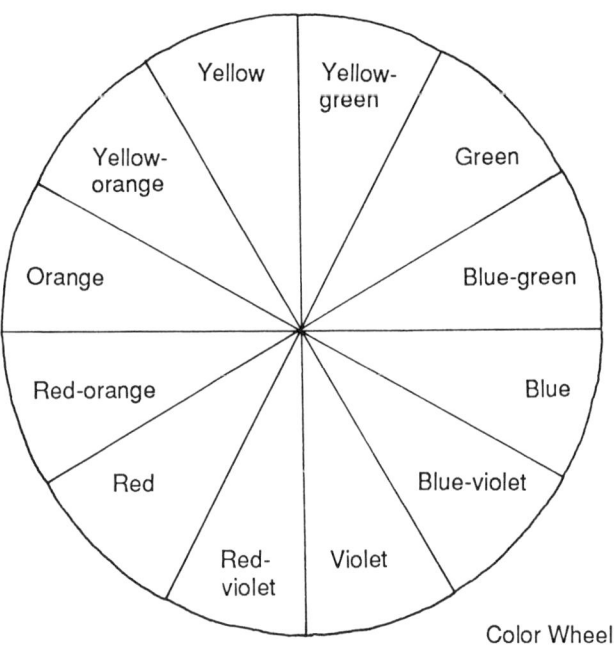

Color Wheel

Form. Flowers and leaves come in many different shapes and sizes (for example, rounded tulips with their spear-shaped leaves), and it is a good idea to make use of these different forms when making a flower arrangement. Often, as is the case with a tulip, the flower's own foliage is contrast enough. But mixing different foliage and flowers is the usual practice to obtain the contrast you are looking for.

Basic Shapes for Arrangements

Beginning an arrangement with a finished design in mind can often be easier than if you have no idea of what the finished product will look like. Many arrangements have basic geometric shapes. If you keep a shape in mind while arranging the flowers your arrangement will come together more quickly.

Many factors help determine what shape to use. Some of these include: the kind of flowers and foliage you are using, where the arrangement will go in the home (a tall arrangement would not work in the center of the dining table), and the size and shape of the container you are using.
Shapes to consider:

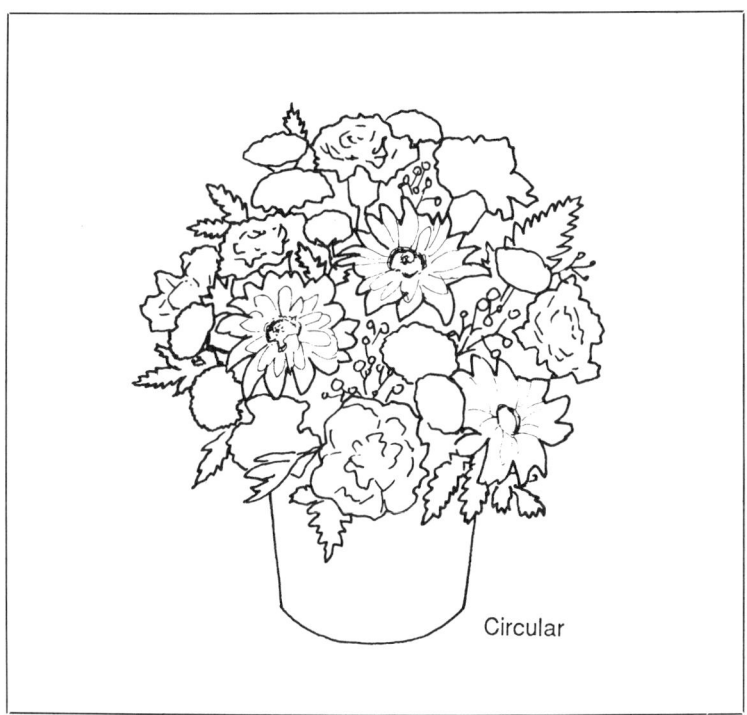

Circular

Circular. This popular shape is satisfying to use and admire. Many round flowers, such as asters and zinnias, work well in this kind of arrangement. One way to avoid a too-round look is to use contrasting foliage with the round flowers.

Symmetrical triangle

Asymmetrical triangle

Triangular. This is a basic shape for many symmetrical arrangements. It can be used with many different variations of height and width and works well with low and wide or tall and narrow containers. The first step is to establish lines of height and width, usually with taller branches of a long-stemmed flower or foliage. Select ones that are paler in color or more delicate in form. Then make a focal point with a large bloom or a group of flowers at the center and just above the rim of the container. Fill in with flowers of different lengths, grouping colors together rather than placing them randomly in the arrangement.

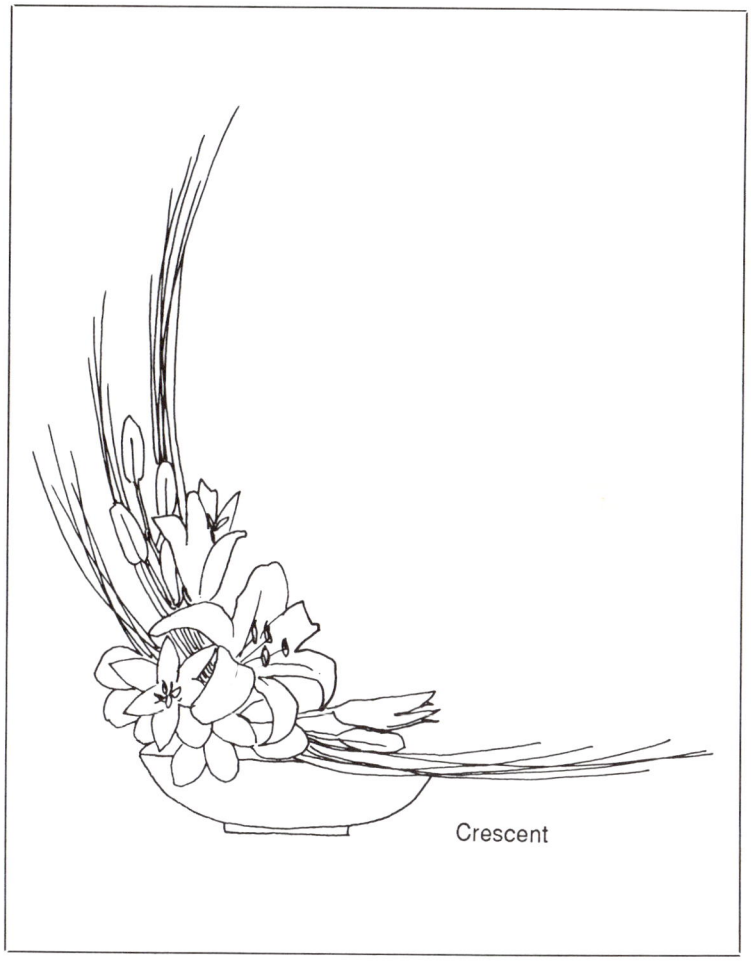

Crescent

Crescent. The crescent is an asymmetrical arrangement that is more difficult to achieve. You need to use flowers with stems that can be bent so you can achieve the curve you are looking for.

Hogarth or S curve   Vertical line arrangement

Line. Line arrangements can also be difficult to do but are worth the extra effort. In modern line arrangements, a branch can be the focal point and the flowers become secondary. A vertical line is useful when you don't have much space for an arrangement. Tall, spiked flowers such as the gladiolus with its own foliage can work well here. Another line arrangement, used a great deal in flower shows, is the Hogarth curve, a rhythmic line in the shape of a long 's' curve. You can achieve it by first using pliable branches to make the curve and then filling in with flowers.

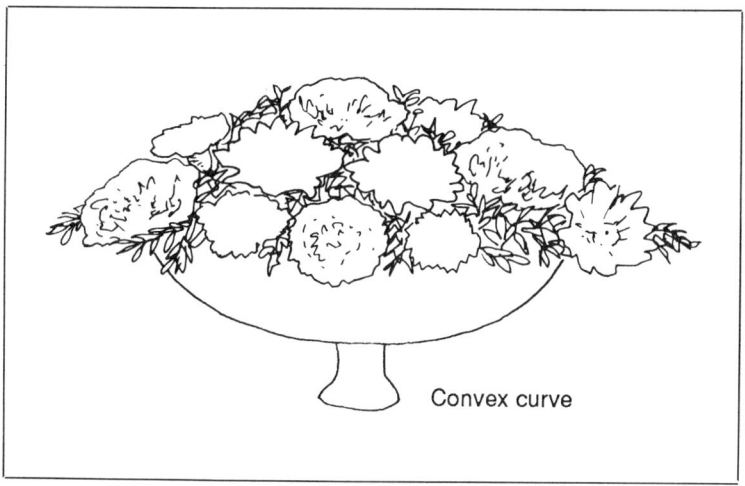
Convex curve

Convex curve. This curve is a good one to use when you make a centerpiece for a table, as it does not have to be tall. The arrangement is symmetrical and should look attractive when viewed from all sides.

Styles of Arrangements

There are many styles of flower arrangements and these are good to know about, though you would probably use a specific style only if you were entering a flower show.

Traditional arrangements include both Occidental and Oriental. Occidental includes all the European "period" styles, including Early American and Colonial Williamsburg. These are mostly mass arrangements, as seen in the paintings by the old Dutch Masters. Oriental arrangements are an art in themselves and often strive for simplicity. Japanese arrangements are usually made around three main lines with some auxiliary lines, cut to very specific proportions. Studying these can help when creating arrangements for the home.

Conventional arrangements are based on geometric form, or line. In some designs, the line is the dominant feature while in others it is used to create shapes such as curves. Additional plant material is brought into many arrangements to strengthen the basic shape. Whereas a true line arrangement may be only one lovely branch and flower, a mass-line or mass arrangement will have many flowers and leaves filling in the basic shape.

Schedules for flower shows usually specify which type of arrangement should be done in the various classes. Size may come into play if a miniature arrangement, perhaps no bigger than 3 inches in any direction, is called for. These are fun to try and can be more of a challenge than a large mass arrangement.

Even if you don't plan on entering flower shows, going to one in your town will give you lots of ideas on what works and what doesn't. You may want to try some ideas of your own. If you do decide to enter a show, watch out! It's easy to become hooked on the art of flower arranging.